JBegin First Sounds
Doudna, Kelly,
India and Iggy /

DAT

FI

# India and Iggy

**Kelly Doudna**

Consulting Editor, Diane Craig, M.A./Reading Specialist

ABDO
Publishing Company

Published by ABDO Publishing Company, 4940 Viking Drive, Edina, Minnesota 55435.

Copyright © 2005 by Abdo Consulting Group, Inc. International copyrights reserved in all countries. No part of this book may be reproduced in any form without written permission from the publisher. SandCastle™ is a trademark and logo of ABDO Publishing Company.

Printed in the United States.

Credits
Edited by: Pam Price
Curriculum Coordinator: Nancy Tuminelly
Cover and Interior Design and Production: Mighty Media
Child Photography: Steven Wewerka, Wewerka Photography
Photo Credits: AbleStock, Brand X Pictures, Kelly Doudna, Photodisc

Library of Congress Cataloging-in-Publication Data

Doudna, Kelly, 1963-
      India and Iggy / Kelly Doudna.
          p. cm. -- (First sounds)
      Includes index.
      ISBN 1-59679-166-7 (hardcover)
      ISBN 1-59679-167-5 (paperback)
         1. English language--Vowels--Juvenile literature. I. Title. II. Series.
   PE1157.D685 2005
   428.1'3--dc22

                                                                                        2004058985

SandCastle™ books are created by a professional team of educators, reading specialists, and content developers around five essential components that include phonemic awareness, phonics, vocabulary, text comprehension, and fluency. All books are written, reviewed, and leveled for guided reading, early intervention reading, and Accelerated Reader® programs and designed for use in shared, guided, and independent reading and writing activities to support a balanced approach to literacy instruction.

## Let Us Know

After reading the book, SandCastle would like you to tell us your stories about reading. What is your favorite page? Was there something hard that you needed help with? Share the ups and downs of learning to read. We want to hear from you! To get posted on the ABDO Publishing Company Web site, send us e-mail at:

**sandcastle@abdopub.com**

**SandCastle Level: Beginning**

## Ii

ABCDEFGH

IJKLMNOPQ

RSTUVWXYZ

abcdefgh

ijklmnopq

rstuvwxyz

# India

**Iggy**

inch

ink

insects

iguana

**instruments**

An  ← is short.

The is black.

Here are the  .

The 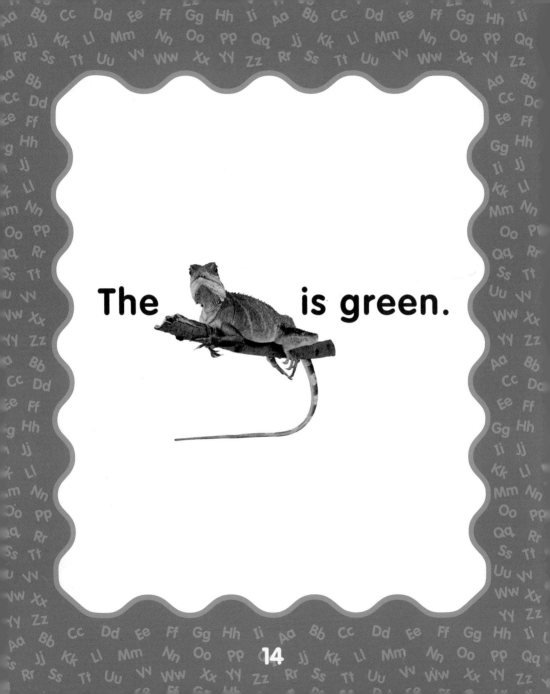 is green.

Here are the .

16

Iggy has ink.

India is in the ink.

India's foot is
8 inches long.

# Which of these pictures begin with i?

# More words that begin with i

if

igloo

ill

in

inside

is

it

its

# About SandCastle™

A professional team of educators, reading specialists, and content developers created the SandCastle™ series to support young readers as they develop reading skills and strategies and increase their general knowledge. The SandCastle™ series has four levels that correspond to early literacy development in young children. The levels are provided to help teachers and parents select the appropriate books for young readers.

**Emerging Readers**
(no flags)

**Beginning Readers**
(1 flag)

**Transitional Readers**
(2 flags)

**Fluent Readers**
(3 flags)

These levels are meant only as a guide. All levels are subject to change.

To see a complete list of SandCastle™ books and other nonfiction titles from ABDO Publishing Company, visit **www.abdopub.com** or contact us at:
4940 Viking Drive, Edina, Minnesota 55435 • 1-800-800-1312 • fax: 1-952-831-1632